LARGE PRINT
KNITTING

LARGE PRINT
KNITTING

JOY GAMMON

A CRESCENT BOOK

This edition © 1986 W.H. Allen & Co Plc
Text copyright © 1986 Joy Gammon
Photographs copyright © 1986 W.H. Allen & Co Plc

First published in 1986 by Crescent Books,
The Large Print Division of W.H. Allen & Co Plc,
44 Hill Street, London W1X 8LB

Photography by Scaioni's Studio Ltd, London

Phototypeset in Plantin by
Phoenix Photosetting, Chatham, Kent
Printed and bound in Great Britain by
Anchor Brendon Ltd, Tiptree, Essex

British Library Cataloguing in Publication Data
Gammon, Joy
    Large print knitting.
    1. Knitting——Patterns
    I. Title
    646.4'07   TT820

    ISBN 1–85188–076–3

For Glad

ACKNOWLEDGEMENTS

All of the yarns used in this book were kindly supplied by: **Lister** Handknitting

of Whiteoak Mills, Westgate, Wakefield WF2 9SF.

Upon receipt of a stamped addressed envelope Lister will be pleased to supply the name of your nearest stockist.

Clothes and accessories for the photographs appearing on the following pages as detailed below:

Page 17: beads by Adrien Mann; skirt by Dickens & Jones; hat by Debenhams.

Page 18: hat by Debenhams; shirt by C17, James Street, W1.

Page 19: trousers and beads by Dickens & Jones; hat by Debenhams.

Page 20: nightdress by D H Evans.

Page 37: blouse, skirt and hat by Mothercare.

Page 56: skirt by Dickens & Jones; blouse by Marks & Spencer; tie by Fenwick of Bond Street.

Page 58: shirt and trousers by C17, James Street, W1; tie by Debenhams.

Page 75: bow by Fenwick of Bond Street; blouse by Marks & Spencer.

CONTENTS LIST

INTRODUCTION

All the patterns in this book have been specially designed to be easy to read and to make, whilst being a mixture of fun, fashionable and classic favourites.

The garments feature simple shaping, which is easier to knit and also has shorter, more straightforward instructions. Wherever possible references from one pattern to another have been avoided, and sizes have been paired so that there are fewer numbers to follow. It is very helpful to mark the size you are working on throughout the pattern, perhaps with a special highlighter pen before you begin. If you do not want to mark the book, why not photocopy the pattern and mark the copy?

The patterns range from a baby's jacket to a man's outdoor jumper, from teenage tops to a comfortable cardigan, and from fashionable to classic. All are in modern yarns, some inexpensive, some more luxurious, but all are in lovely colours. Throughout, stitch patterns which look striking and attractive but which are easy to follow and to knit have been chosen.

The individual patterns give both the familiar inch size range and the centimetre size range, otherwise centimetres only have been used to avoid long lines of figures. The Introduction includes a needle-size conversion chart in case your knitting needles are a mixture of old numbers and new millimetre sizes. The major abbreviations are all the familiar ones. They are listed in the Introduction only, with occasional special abbreviations in the pattern to which they refer.

Whatever your age, beginner or not, if you need clear, easy to use patterns, this is the book for you.

ABBREVIATIONS

beg = beginning   rem = remaining
cont = continue   sl = slip
dec = decrease(ing)   st(s) = stitch(es)
foll = follows(ing)   st. st. = stocking stitch (one row knit,
inc = increase   one row purl)
K = knit   tbl = through back of loop
P = purl   tog = together
patt = pattern   yon = yarn over needle

KNITTING NEEDLE SIZES

Original UK	000	00	0	1	2	3
Metric (mm)	9	8½	8	7½	7	6½
USA	15	13	–	11	10½	10

Original UK	4	5	6	7	8	9
Metric (mm)	6	5½	5	4½	4	3½ & 3¾
USA	9	8	7	6	5	4

Original UK	10	11	12	13	14
Metric (mm)	3¼	2¾ & 3	2½	2¼	2
USA	3	2	1	0	00

BRITISH AND AMERICAN KNITTING TERMS

UK	US
stocking stitch =	stockinette stitch
tension =	gauge
work straight =	work even
cast off =	bind off
yarn over needle =	yarn over

YOUNG
FASHION
CABLE

YOUNG FASHION CABLE

(Colour illustration, page 17)

An Aran with a difference, this bright warm jumper has the traditional cables in a simple, modern shape, with dropped sleeves, a cable on the sleeve too and a polo neck. An added bonus is that this Aran yarn will machine wash.

MATERIALS

Lister Machine Washable Aran
Green (3226)   15   15   16   17 × 40g balls

1 pr 5mm (No. 6) needles
1 pr 4½mm (No. 7) needles
1 pr 4mm (No. 8) needles
Cable needle.

MEASUREMENTS

To fit	76–81	86–91	97–102	107–112 cm
	30–32	34–36	38–40	42–44 in.

TENSION

18 sts and 22 rows = 10cm (4in.) in stocking stitch on 5mm (No. 6) needles.

Special abbreviation: C8B = place next 4 sts on a cable needle at back of work, K4, then K4 from cable needle.

BACK

With 4mm needles cast on 76(84,96,104) sts and work 8cm in K2, P2 rib.
Keeping rib correct, work next (increasing) row as follows:
Rib 12(16,21,24), inc 1 st in rib in each of the next 6 sts,
rib 40(40,42,44) sts, inc 1 st in rib in each of the next 6 sts, rib rem 12(16,21,24) sts. (88,96,108,116 sts.)
Change to 5mm needles and pattern, working establishing row for cables as follows: K12(16,21,24), P2, K8, P2, K40(40,42,44), P2, K8, P2, K rem 12(16,21,24).
From now on, work in st. st. in all areas except the 2 st bands of rev st. st., either side of each 8 st cable band of st. st.
Work 11 further rows in this way, ending with a wrong side row.
Next row. K12(16,21,24), P2, C8B, P2, K40(40,42,44), P2, C8B, P2, K rem 12(16,21,24). ⋆
Continue in this way, cabling on every 12th row, until work measures 61(64,66,69)cm ending with a wrong side row.
Next row. K12(16,21,24), P2 tog, (K2 tog) 4 times, P2 tog, K40(40,42,44), P2 tog, (K2 tog) 4 times, P2 tog, K rem 12(16,21,24) sts. (76,84,96,104 sts.)
Next row. Cast off 22(26,31,34) sts, P until 22(26,31,34) sts rem, place the 32(32,34,36) sts just worked onto a holder, cast off to end.

FRONT

Work as given for Back as far as *.
Continue in this way, cabling on every 12th row, until work measures 52(55,56,58)cm, ending with a wrong side row.
Keeping cable correct, shape neck as follows:
Next row. Work 36(40,46,50) sts, turn, P2 tog tbl, work back to end.
** Working on these sts only, dec 1 st at neck edge only on next 3(3,4,4) rows, then on every alt row until 28(32,37,40) sts rem. Work straight until armhole edge matches that on the Back, ending with a wrong side row.**
Next row. K12(16,21,24), P2 tog, (K2 tog) 4 times, P2 tog, K rem 4 sts. (22,26,31,34 sts.)
Cast off.
With right side facing, rejoin yarn to inside edge of rem sts, K16 sts and place them on a holder, work to end.
Next row. Work to last 2 sts, P2 tog.
Rep from ** to **.
Next row. K4, P2 tog, (K2 tog) 4 times, P2 tog, K rem 12(16,21,24) sts. (22,26,31,34 sts.)
Cast off.

SLEEVES

With 4mm needles, cast on 40(44,44,48) sts and work 6cm in K2, P2 rib.
Keeping rib correct, work next (increasing) row as follows:
Rib 17(19,19,21), inc 1 st in rib in each of the next 6 sts,

rib rem 17(19,19,21) sts. (46,50,50,54 sts.)
Change to 5mm needles and pattern, working establishing row
for cable: K17(19,19,21), P2, K8, P2, K rem 17(19,19,21) sts.
From now on, keep cable correct as before on these centre 12 sts,
working centre 8 sts as C8B on every foll 12th row as before.
At the same time, inc 1 st at each end of every 3rd row until
there are 82(88,92,96) sts, working all increases into the st. st. at
either side of the single centre cable.
Continuing to keep cable correct, work straight until sleeve
measures 46(46,48,48)cm, or desired length to underarm, ending
with a wrong side row.
Next row. K35(38,40,42), P2 tog, (K2 tog) 4 times, P2 tog,
K rem 35(38,40,42) sts.
Cast off loosely.

NECKBAND

Press according to ball band instructions, avoiding the cables.
Matching all pattern, join left shoulder seam.
With 4mm needles and with right side facing, pick up and K the
32(32,34,36) sts from the Back neck holder, 18(18,19,20) sts
down the left neck slope, the 16 sts from the Front neck holder,
and 18(18,19,20) sts up the right neck slope. (84,84,88,92 sts.)
Work in K2, P2 rib until neck rib measures 3cm.
Change to 4½mm needles and work a further 5cm in K2, P2 rib.
Change to 5mm needles and work a further 10cm in K2, P2 rib.
(Neck rib now measures 18cm.)
Cast off very loosely in rib.

TO MAKE UP

Join rem seams matching pattern, ensuring that centre of sleeve cable matches shoulder seam, and that armholes are 22(23,24,25)cm deep after making up.

For
pattern
see page 11

17

For
pattern
see page 65

18

For pattern see page 25

For pattern see page 21

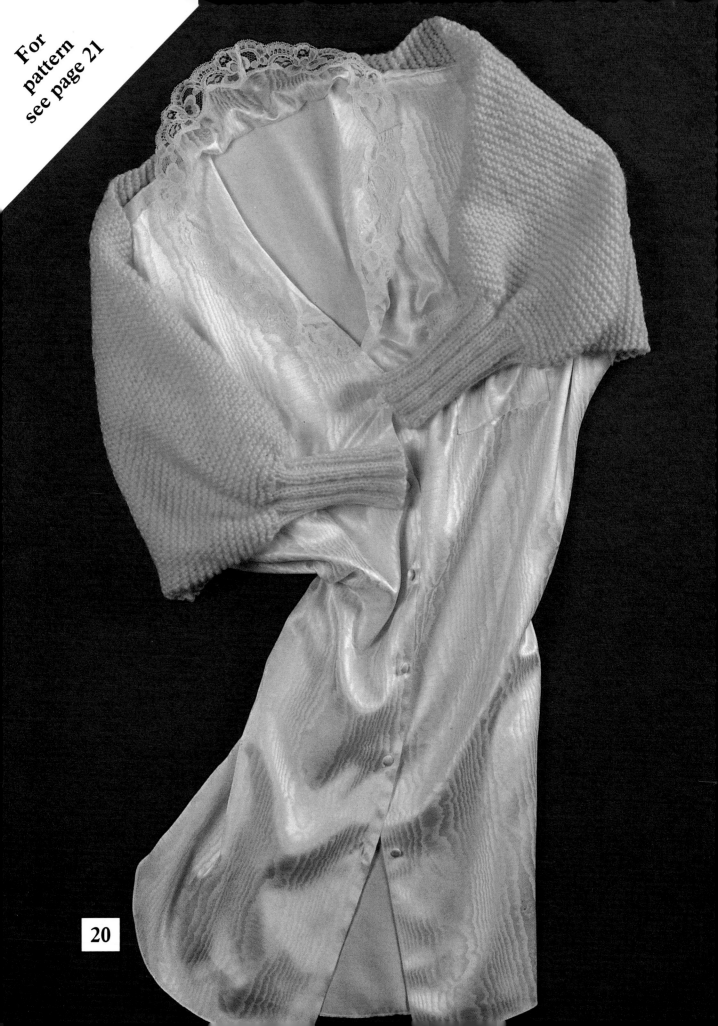

SHAWL/
STOLE

SHAWL/STOLE

(Colour illustration, page 20)

This wrap is very easy to knit and to wear. It is like a stole with cuffs and is wonderfully warm, especially to wear in bed. Knit it in a brushed chunky yarn like Lister's Libra or, alternatively, use a fancy evening yarn to make a party cover-up.

MATERIALS

Lister Libra in Pink (109)   3 × 100g balls
or Lister Shalimar Shimmer in Grey (933) 7 × 25g balls

1 pr 6½mm (No. 3) needles
1 pr 5½mm (No. 5) needles
1 pr 5mm (No. 6) needles

MEASUREMENTS

One size fits all. The shawl is approximately 56cm (22in.) wide and 137cm (54in.) long in total.

TENSION

13 sts and 24 rows = 10cm (4in.) in garter stitch (every row knit) in both yarns, on 6½mm (No. 3) needles.

MADE IN ONE PIECE

With 5mm needles, cast on 36 sts and work 7½cm in K2, P2 rib.
Change to 5½mm needles and cont in K2, P2 rib to a total measurement of 15cm.
Change to 6½mm needles and garter st (every row knit), and inc 1 st in every st on the first row. (72 sts.)
Work straight in garter st to a total measurement of 122cm from the cast-on edge.
Next row. (K2 tog) to end. (36 sts.)
Change to 5½mm needles and work 7½cm in K2, P2 rib.
Change to 5mm needles and continue in K2, P2 rib until rib measures 15cm.
Cast off loosely in rib.

TO MAKE UP

Do not press. Brush if preferred.
Seam the cuff ribs only.

COTTON VEST

COTTON VEST

(Colour illustration, page 19)

Make this cotton vest for hot summer days. It is short with deep armholes and a deep round neck. The bottom edge has a hem threaded with a cord-tie, and the top edges have a garter stitch border to avoid any necessity for picking up.

MATERIALS

Lister Bamboo
Turquoise (783)   5   5   6 × 50g balls

1 pr 4mm (No. 8) needles
Optional length of cord or ribbon for waist drawstring.

MEASUREMENTS

To fit   76–81   86–91   97–102 cm
                   30–32   34–36   38–40 in.

TENSION

22 sts and 28 rows = 10cm (4in.) in stocking stitch on 4mm (No. 8) needles.

BACK

With 4mm needles, cast on 95(105,115) sts and work 6 rows in st. st. starting with a K row.

P 1 row.

Continue in st. st. starting with a P row, and work straight to a total measurement of 27(28,29)cm ending with a K row.

Begin garter stitch edges as follows:

Next row. K6, P to last 6, K6.

Next row. K.

Next row. K8, P to last 8, K8.

Next row. K.

Next row. K10, P to last 10, K10.

Shape armholes.

Next row. Cast off 6 sts, K to end.

Next row. Cast off 6 sts, K until there are 4 sts on the right hand needle, P to last 4, K4.

These 4 edge sts will remain in K on every row throughout rem of work.

Continue to shape armholes:

Next row. K4, K2 tog, K to last 6, K2 tog tbl, K4.

Next row. K4, P2 tog tbl, P to last 6, P2 tog, K4.

Rep these 2 rows 2(4,6) more times. (71,73,75) sts rem. *

Keeping 4 sts in K at each end of every row, work 21 rows straight.

** **Begin neck border.**

Next row. K4, P19(20,21), K25, P19(20,21), K rem 4.

Next row. K.
Next row. K4, P17(18,19), K29, P17(18,19), K rem 4.
Next row. K.
Next row. K4, P15(16,17), K33, P15(16,17), K rem 4.

Shape neck.
Next row. K23(24,25), cast off 25, K rem 23(24,25).
Working on right neck side only:
Next row. K4, P to last 6, P2 tog, K4.
Next row. K4, K2 tog, K to end.
Repeat these 2 rows once more.
Next row. K4, P to last 6, P2 tog, K4.
Next row. K.
Rep these 2 rows until 14 sts rem.
Keeping 4 sts in K at each end of every row, work straight until armholes measure 23(24,25)cm ending with a wrong side row.
Cast off.

With wrong side of work facing, rejoin yarn to neck edge of rem sts and work as follows:
Next row. K4, P2 tog tbl, P to last 4, K4.
Next row. K to last 6, K2 tog tbl, K4.
Repeat these 2 rows once more.
Next row. K4, P2 tog tbl, P to last 4, K4.
Next row. K.
Repeat these 2 rows until 14 sts rem.
Complete to match first side.
Cast off.

FRONT

Work as given for Back as far as *.
Work next row, K4, P to last 4, K4.
Work as given for Back from ** to end, so omitting the 20 straight rows and thus lowering the front neck.

TO MAKE UP

Press according to ball band instructions.
Join top straps and side seams, leaving about 1cm opening immediately above the reverse hem row at the bottom of the right side seam. Turn this hem onto wrong side and loosely slip stitch down. Make a plait or cord or, using a bought ribbon or cord, thread the bottom hem and tie.

CHILD'S TRADITIONAL FAIR-ISLE CARDIGAN

CHILD'S TRADITIONAL FAIR-ISLE CARDIGAN

(Colour illustration, page 37)

Fair Isle is easy to do from our clear chart and the simple repeat, worked in a speckled red yarn on cream, looks striking and much more difficult than it really is. A raglan V-necked cardigan is perfect for parties or play.

MATERIALS

Lister Richmond double-knitting		
Cream (3158)	4	4 × 50g balls
Lister Richmond Tweed double-knitting		
Red (4002)	1	1 × 50g ball

1 pr 4mm (No. 8) needles
1 pr 3¼mm (No. 10) needles
5(6) buttons.

MEASUREMENTS

To fit	56–61	66–71 cm
	22–24	26–28 in.

32

TENSION

24 sts and 32 rows = 10cm (4in.) in stocking stitch and Fair Isle on 4mm (No. 8) needles.

BACK

With 3¼mm needles and cream, cast on 78(90) sts and work 12 rows in K1, P1 rib.
Change to 4mm needles and st. st. and work 2 rows.
Join in red.
Next row [Commencing Fair-Isle border]. In K, work * 1 st red, 4 sts cream, 1 st red *, repeat from * to * to end.
This row becomes row 1 of the chart.

X		X	X		X	8 ← Row Numbers
X					X	7
	X			X		6
		X	X			5
	X			X		4
		X	X			3
	X			X		2
X					X	1

6st repeat

X = Contrast (Red)

All rem sts Cream

Continue in st. st. and Fair-Isle pattern, working the 6 sts repeat from the chart and working the 7 further st. st. rows to complete the chart, beginning with row 2 in P.

Repeat rows 1–7 of the chart once more.

Continue in st. st. in plain cream until work measures 25(32)cm ending with a P row.

Shape raglan.

Cast off 3 sts at beg of next 2 rows.

Next row. K2, K2 tog tbl, K to last 4, K2 tog, K2.

Next row. K1, P to last st, K1.

Repeat these 2 rows until 24(28) sts rem.

Cast off.

RIGHT FRONT

With 3¼mm needles and cream, cast on 42(48) sts and work 12 rows in K1, P1 rib.

Change to 4mm needles and st. st. and work 2 rows.

Work the 15 rows of Fair Isle in the same way as before.

Work straight in plain cream until Front measures same as Back to armhole, ending with a K row. ★★

Shape raglan and neck.

Next row. Cast off 3 sts, P to end.

Next row. K1, K2 tog tbl, K to last 4, K2 tog, K2.

Next row. K1, P to end.

★★★ Repeat these 2 rows until 11(11) sts rem.

Keeping neck edge straight, dec 1 st in the same way as before at

the raglan edge only of every K row until 2 sts rem.
Work 2 tog.
Fasten off.

LEFT FRONT

Work as given for Right Front as far as **.

Shape raglan and neck.
P1 row, so ending at armhole edge.
Next row. Cast off 3 sts, K to end.
Next row. P to last st, K1.
Next row. K2, K2 tog tbl, K to last 3, K2 tog, K1.
Next row. P to last st, K1.
Work as given for Right Front from *** to end.

SLEEVES

With 3¼mm needles and cream, cast on 42(42) sts and work 16
rows in K1, P1 rib.
Change to 4mm needles and st. st. and work 2 rows in cream.
Join in red.
Commence Fair-Isle border in the same way as given for the Back
and work the 8 rows from the chart, followed by rows 1–7 again.
At the same time, inc 1 st at each end of the 3rd row of the chart,
then every foll 6th row until there are 60(68) sts.
Continuing in cream when the 15 Fair-Isle rows are complete,
work straight to a total length of 28(36)cm or desired length to
underarm.

Shape raglan.
Cast off 3 sts at beg of next 2 rows.
Repeat the 2 raglan shaping rows as given for the Back until 6 sts rem.
Cast off.

FRONTBAND

With 3¼mm needles and cream, cast on 8 sts and work 2 rows of K1, P1 rib.

Make buttonholes.
Next row. Rib 3, cast off 2, rib to end.
Next row. Rib 3, cast on 2, rib to end.
Continue in rib making further buttonholes in the same way at 5cm intervals until 5(6) have been worked.
Continue in rib without further buttonholes until band, when slightly stretched, reaches from the bottom of the welt, up one front, round the back neck and down the other front to the bottom of the welt.
Cast off in rib.

TO MAKE UP

Press according to ball band instructions.
Join seams matching all shaping and pattern.
Sew front band into position with buttonholes on the chosen side.
Stitch on buttons to match buttonholes.

For
pattern
see page 31

37

For
pattern
see page 39

CHILD'S STRIPED JUMPER

CHILD'S STRIPED JUMPER

(Colour illustration, page 38)

This jumper is in the brightest stripes imaginable and is easy enough for the teenage wearer to knit for herself. It has a simple ribbed slashed neck and dropped shoulders making the style easy.

MATERIALS

Lister Richmond double-knitting

Yellow (3227)	2	2	3 × 50g balls
Blue (680)	2	2	3 × 50g balls
Red (2754)	2	2	3 × 50g balls

1 pr 4mm (No. 8) needles
1 pr 3¼mm (No. 10) needles.

MEASUREMENTS

To fit	56–61	66–71	76–81 cm
	22–24	26–28	30–32 in.

TENSION

24 sts and 32 rows = 10cm (4in.) in stocking stitch on 4mm (No. 8) needles.

BACK AND FRONT [Both alike]

With 3¼mm needles and red, cast on 78(90,102) sts and work 14 rows of K1, P1 rib.

Change to 4mm needles and blue, and st. st. and work 12 rows in blue, starting with a K row.

Work next 12 rows in yellow.

Work next 12 rows in red.

Rep these 36 rows until work measures a total of 37(46,53)cm ending after any complete stripe with a P row.

Change to the next colour in the sequence and, keeping the sequence correct, K 1 row.

Remaining on 4mm needles, work 11 rows in this colour in K1, P1 rib.

Cast off in rib.

SLEEVES

With 3¼mm needles and red, cast on 44(46,48) sts and work 14 rows in K1, P1 rib.

Change to 4mm needles, st. st. and blue and work in 12-row stripes in the same colour sequence as given for the Back.

At the same time, inc 1 st at each end of the 3rd then every foll 4th(4th,5th) row until there are 72(84,90) sts.

Work straight in stripes in colour sequence until sleeve measures 28(36,46)cm or desired length to underarm, ending with a P row and after a complete stripe.

Cast off loosely.

TO MAKE UP

Press according to ball band instructions.
Join all seams matching all stripes and leaving a neck opening 17(18,19)cm wide, and armholes 15(18,19)cm deep after making up.

TRADITIONAL CLASSIC CARDIGAN

TRADITIONAL CLASSIC CARDIGAN

(Colour illustration, page 56)

A cardigan in the traditional style with set-in sleeves, a V-neck and pockets. The pattern is as easy as possible and goes up to size 122cm (48in.), so all the family can have one.

MATERIALS

Lister Richmond double-knitting
Jade (3218)   8   9   10   10 × 50g balls

1 pr 4mm (No. 8) needles
1 pr 3¼mm (No. 10) needles
5 buttons.

MEASUREMENTS

To fit	86–91	97–102	107–112	117–122 cm
	34–36	38–40	42–44	46–48 in.

TENSION

24 sts and 32 rows = 10cm (4in.) in stocking stitch on 4mm (No. 8) needles.

BACK

With 3¼mm needles, cast on 114(126,138,150) sts and work 4(4,5,5)cm in K1, P1 rib.
Change to 4mm needles and st. st. and work straight to a total measurement of 38(41,43,43)cm or desired length to underarm, ending with a P row.

Shape armholes.

Cast off 2(3,4,4) sts at beg of next 2 rows.
Dec 1 st at each end of next 7 rows, then every alt row until 88(96,104, 112) sts rem.
Work straight until armholes measure 19(20,22,23)cm, ending with a P row.

Shape shoulders.

Cast off 7(8,8,9) sts at beg of next 6 rows, then 7(6,8,8) sts at beg of next 2 rows.
Cast off rem 32(36,40,42) sts.

POCKET LININGS [Make 2]

With 4mm needles cast on 33(35,37,39) sts.
Work in st. st. for 11cm, ending with a P row.
Slip sts onto a holder.

LEFT FRONT

With 3¼mm needles, cast on 54(60,66,72) sts and work
4(4,5,5)cm in K1, P1 rib.
Change to 4mm needles and st. st. and work straight to a total
measurement of 14cm, ending with a P row. ★

Place pocket.
Next row. K10(12,14,16), (P1, K1) to last 14(16,18,20) sts, P1,
K to end.
Work 6 further rows, keeping pocket rib correct and working
st. st. at either side, ending with a right side row.
Next row. P12(14,16,18), cast off next 33(35,37,39) sts in rib, P
to end.
★★Next row [Right side facing]. K to pocket opening, K across
the 33(35,37,39) sts of one pocket lining, K to end.
Continue in st. st. until Front measures 8 rows less than Back to
armhole shaping, so ending with a P row and ending at armhole
edge.

Shape neck.
Dec 1 st at end of next row, and also at end of foll 4th row.
Work 3 rows straight, ending at armhole edge.

Shape armhole.
Next row. Cast off 2(3,4,4) sts, work to last 2, work 2 tog.
Continue to dec 1 st at neck edge on every 4th row, and at the
same time, dec 1 st at armhole edge on next 7 rows, then on every
alt row 4(5,6,8) times. (35,38,42,45 sts rem.)
Keeping armhole edge straight, cont to dec at neck edge on every

4th row as before until 28(30,32,35) sts rem.
Work straight until armhole measures same as on Back, ending at armhole edge.
Cast off 7(8,8,9) sts at beg of next and every alt row until 7(6,8,8) sts rem.
Work 1 row.
Cast off.

RIGHT FRONT

Work as given for Left Front as far as *.

Place pockets.
Next row. K13(15,17,19), (P1, K1) to last 11(13,15,17) sts, P1, K to end.
Work 6 further rows, keeping pocket rib correct and working st. st. at either side, ending with a right side row.
Next row. P9(11,13,15), cast off next 33(35,37,39) sts in rib, P to end.
Work as given for Left Front from ** to end, but, work 1 further row before commencing neck shaping, ending at armhole edge before commencing neck and armhole shaping.

SLEEVES

With 3¼mm needles, cast on 50(54,58,62) sts and work 5cm in K1, P1 rib.

Change to 4mm needles and st. st. and inc 1 st at each end of the 5th, then every foll 9th(8th,7th,7th) row until there are 76(84,92,100) sts.
Work straight to a total length of 46(47,47,48)cm or desired length to underarm, ending with a P row.

Shape top.
Cast off 2(3,4,4) sts at beg of next 2 rows.
Dec 1 st at each end of next 5 rows, then every alt row until 38(42,46,50) sts rem.
Dec 1 st at each end of the next 6 rows.
Cast off 4 sts at the beg of the next 2 rows.
Cast off rem 18(22,26,30) sts.

TO MAKE UP AND BANDS

Press according to ball band instructions.
Join all seams matching all shapings.
Slip stitch pocket linings into place.

Buttonband.
With 3¼mm needles, cast on 12 sts and work in K1, P1 rib until band, when slightly stretched, reaches from bottom of welt, up neck slope, across the back neck and down the other neck slope to a point 1cm below commencement of neck shaping.
Mark positions on band for 5 buttons, one 1cm below commencement of neck shaping, one 2.5cm above cast-on edge and the rem 3 evenly spaced between.

Complete band to match other side, working buttonholes opposite marked points as follows:

Next row. Rib 4, cast off in rib until 4 sts rem, rib to end.

Next row. Rib casting on 4 sts above the 4 sts cast off on the previous row.

Cast off when band is complete.

Attach band with buttonholes on the chosen side.

Stitch on buttons to match.

BLUE AND WHITE STRIPED JUMPER

BLUE AND WHITE STRIPED JUMPER

(Colour illustration, page 55)

It's very easy to do this spectacular pattern and there is no picture (intarsia) knitting involved. The shaped stripes are made by working part rows. The basic jumper is very simple with a ribbed slash neck and plain dropped sleeves, and the yarn is machine washable pure wool. The jumper is quite long, so work one less pattern repeat if you prefer a shorter line.

MATERIALS

Lister Motoravia Superwash double knitting pure wool.

Blue (1652)	9	9	10 × 50g balls
White (1661)	4	4	4 × 50g balls

1 pr 4mm (No. 8) needles
1 pr 3¼mm (No. 10) needles.

MEASUREMENTS

To fit	76–81	86–91	97–102 cm
	30–32	34–36	38–40 in.

TENSION

24 sts and 32 rows = 10cm (4in.) in stocking stitch on 4mm (No. 8) needles.

BACK AND FRONT [Both alike]

With 3¼mm needles and blue, cast on 102(114,126) sts and work 6cm in K1, P1 rib.
Change to 4mm needles and K 1 row in blue.
Change to white and commence pattern:
*Next row. In white P77(86,95), turn, sl 1, K back.
Next row. P51(57,63), turn, sl 1, K back.
Next row. P25(28,31), turn, sl 1, K back.
P 1 row.
Change to blue.
In blue, K 1 row, then P 1 row.
Next row. K25(28,31), turn, sl 1, P back.
Next row. K51(57,63), turn, sl 1, P back.
Next row. K77(86,95), turn, sl 1, P back.
Next row. K51(57,63), turn, sl 1, P back.
Next row. K25(28,31), turn, sl 1, P back.
K 1 row.
Change to white.
In white, P 1 row, then K 1 row.
Next row. P25(28,31), turn, sl 1, K back.
Next row. P51(57,63), turn, sl 1, K back. *
Repeat from * to * 10(11,11) times. Work should now measure 56(63,63)cm.

Change to blue and P 1 row.
Next row. K22(28,32), (K1, P1) until 22(28,32) sts rem, K to end.
Next row. P22(28,32), (K1, P1) until 22(28,32) sts rem, P to end.
Repeat these 2 rows 5 more times, so working centre rib on 12 rows in all.
Work should now measure 60(67,67)cm.
Cast off loosely in st. st. on either shoulder and in rib on the centre section.

SLEEVES [Both alike, in blue throughout]

With 3¼mm needles, cast on 54(56,58) sts and work 6cm in K1, P1 rib.
Change to 4mm needles and st. st. and inc 1 st at each end of the 5th, then every foll 4th row until there are 96(102,108) sts.
Work straight to a total length of 46(46,47)cm or desired length to underarm.
Cast off loosely.

TO MAKE UP

Press according to ball band instructions.
Make up all seams, leaving ribbed section open to form the neck, and ensuring that the armholes are 20(22,23)cm deep after making up.

54

For pattern see page 51

For pattern see page 43

56

For
pattern
see page 83

For
pattern
see page 59

58

MAN'S
SLIP-OVER

MAN'S SLIP-OVER

(Colour illustration, page 58)

Knit a man's classic slip-over in favourite yellow. Or try cricket white or bright colours. The V-neck is a wrapover to avoid fiddly shaping, and the traditional style is smart and comfortable with or without a jacket.

MATERIALS

Lister Easy Wash Crepe double-knitting
Yellow (3208)   8   8   9 × 40g balls

1 pr 4mm (No. 8) needles
1 pr 3¼mm (No. 10) needles
A 3¼mm circular needle of medium length.

MEASUREMENTS

To fit	91–97	102–107	112–117 cm
	36–38	40–42	44–46 in.

TENSION

24 sts and 32 rows = 10cm (4in.) in stocking stitch on 4mm (No. 8) needles.

BACK

With 3¼mm needles, cast on 120(132,144) sts and work 6cm in K1, P1 rib.
Change to 4mm needles and st. st. and work straight to a total measurement of 38(41,43)cm ending with a P row.

Shape armholes.
Cast off 6(8,9) sts at beg of next 2 rows. (108,116,126 sts.)
Dec 1 st at each end of the next 3 rows, then every alt row until 96(104,114) sts rem, ending with a K row.
P 1 row. *
Work straight until armholes measure 23(23,24)cm, ending with a P row.

Shape shoulders.
Cast off 9(10,11) sts at beg of next 6 rows.
Place the rem 42(44,48) sts on a holder.

FRONT

Work as given for Back as far as *.

Shape neck.
Next row. K48(52,57), turn, P2 tog tbl, and P back.
** Working on these sts only, dec 1 st at neck edge only of every foll K row until 27(30,33) sts rem.
Work straight until armholes measure same as on Back to shoulder, ending at armhole edge.

Shape shoulder.
Cast off 9(10,11) sts at beg of next row.
Work 1 row.
Repeat these 2 rows once more.
Cast off rem 9(10,11) sts.★★
Rejoin yarn to inside edge of rem sts, K to end.
Next row. P to last 2, P2 tog.
Rep from ★★ to ★★.

NECKBAND

Press according to ball band instructions.
Join both shoulder seams matching shaping.
With the 3¼mm circular needle and beginning at the centre
neck, with right side facing, pick up and K 50(50,54) sts evenly
up the right front neck slope, the 42(44,48) sts from the back
neck holder, and 50(50,54) sts evenly down the left front neck
slope. (142,144,156 sts.)
Work 12 rows in K1, P1 rib, working in both directions, **not** in
the round.
Cast off loosely in rib.

ARMBANDS

With 3¼mm needles, and with right side facing, pick up and K
the 6(8,9) sts cast off at the bottom of the armhole, 53(53,56) sts
evenly up one side of the armhole to the shoulder seam,
53(53,56) sts evenly down the other side to the cast off sts, and

the rem 6(8,9) cast off sts at the bottom of the armhole.
(118,122,130 sts.)
Work 10 rows in K1, P1 rib.
Cast off loosely in rib.

TO MAKE UP

Join rem seams, fold neckband ends left over right, and invisibly catch down the ends only to the V.

MAN'S
CHUNKY RIB

MAN'S CHUNKY RIB

(Colour illustration, page 18)

Knit a warm jumper in chunky moss stitch rib, with raglan sleeves and a round neck. It is ideal for outdoor hobbies or pottering in the garden.

MATERIALS

Lister Chunky in Fawn (1080) 23   24   26 × 50g balls

1 pr 6½mm (No. 3) needles
1 pr 5½mm (No. 5) needles.

MEASUREMENTS

To fit	97–102	107–112	117–122 cm
	38–40	42–44	46–48 in.

TENSION

14 sts and 20 rows = 10cm (4in.) in stocking stitch on 6½mm (No. 3) needles.

BACK

With 5½mm needles, cast on 72(80,88) sts and work 8cm in K2, P2 rib.

Next (increasing) row. Keeping rib correct, rib 15(4,12),⋆ inc 1 st in next st in rib, rib 2(3,3) ⋆, rep from ⋆ to ⋆ to end. (91,99,107 sts.)

Change to 6½mm needles and work rib pattern as follows:

Row 1. K3, (P1, K3) to end.

Row 2. K1, (P1, K3) to last 2, P1, K1.

Rep these 2 rows throughout, thus creating a moss stitch rib. Work straight in rib, until work measures 48cm or desired length to underarm, ending with a **Row 2**.

Shape raglan.

(Working all dec sts into the pattern, and so keeping rib correct), cast off 4 sts at beg of next 2 rows. (83,91,99 sts.)

Next row. K2 tog, pattern to last 2, K2 tog tbl.

Next row. K1, pattern to last st, K1.

Rep these 2 rows until 57(59,61) sts rem, ending with the wrong side (2nd) row. ⋆

Next row. K2 tog, pattern to last 2, K2 tog tbl.

Next row. K2 tog tbl, pattern to last 2, K2 tog.

Rep these 2 rows until 29(31,33) sts rem.

Leave these sts on a holder for back neck.

FRONT

Work as given for Back as far as ⋆.

Shape neck [Keeping rib pattern correct throughout].
Next row. K2 tog, pattern 19(19,19), turn, P2 tog tbl, pattern to last 2, K2 tog.
★★ Working on these sts only, continue to dec at raglan edge on every row in the same way as on the Back. **At the same time**, dec 1 st at neck edge on next 3 rows, then on next 3 alt rows.
Continuing to dec at raglan edge on every row, work neck edge straight until 2 sts rem.
Work 2 tog, fasten off. ★★
Rejoin yarn to inside edge of rem sts.
Pattern 15(17,19) sts and place them on a holder, pattern to last 2, K2 tog tbl.
Next row. K2 tog tbl, pattern to last 2, P2 tog.
Rep from ★★ to ★★.

SLEEVES

With 5½mm needles, cast on 32(32,36) sts and work 6cm in K2, P2 rib.
Next (increasing) row. Keeping rib correct, inc 1 st in first st in rib, rib 1(1,5), ★ inc 1 st in next st in rib, rib 2★, rep from ★ to ★ to end. (43,43,47 sts.)

Change to 6½mm needles and rib stitch pattern as given for the Back and, working all increases into the pattern, inc 1 st at each end of every 3rd row until there are 77(89,99) sts.
Work straight, keeping pattern correct until sleeve measures 46(48,51)cm ending with a wrong side (2nd) row.

Shape raglan [Keeping rib pattern correct throughout].
Cast off 4 sts at beg of next 2 rows. (69,81,91 sts.)
Dec 1 st at each end of every alt row in the same way as given for the Back until there are 53(63,71) sts, ending with a wrong side row.
Dec 1 st at each end of every row in the same way as given for the Back until there are 5(7,7) sts.
Leave these sts on a holder.

NECKBAND

Do not press. Join both front and the left back raglan seams matching the underarm shaping.
With 5½mm needles and right side facing, pick up and knit the 29(31,33) sts from the back neck holder, 5(7,7) sts from the left sleeve top, working 2 tog in the centre, 14 sts down the left neck slope, the 15(17,19) sts from the front neck holder, 14 sts up the right neck slope, and 5(7,7) sts from the right sleeve top working 2 tog in the centre. (80,88,92 sts.)
Work 8 rows of K2, P2 rib, ending with a right side row.
K1 row.
Work 7 further rows of K2, P2 rib, keeping rib correct.
Cast off very loosely in rib.

TO MAKE UP

Make up rem seams matching all shaping.
Turn neckband onto wrong side and loosely slip stitch down.

ARAN FASHION SLIP-OVER

ARAN FASHION SLIP-OVER

(Colour illustration, page 75)

Rich scarlet wool makes this simple slip-over something warm and special. A fairly deep neck and dropped shoulders make for easy and quick knitting for a practical and fashionable cover-up.

MATERIALS

Lister Pure Wool Aran
Red (2238)   9   9   10 × 50g balls

1 pr 5mm (No. 6) needles
1 pr 4mm (No. 8) needles.

MEASUREMENTS

To fit   76–81   86–91   97–102 cm
            30–32   34–36   38–40 in.

TENSION

18 sts and 22 rows = 10cm (4in.) in stocking stitch on 5mm (No. 6) needles.

BACK

With 4mm needles, cast on 76(88,96) sts and work 8cm in K2, P2 rib.*
Change to 5mm needles and st. st. and work straight to a total measurement of 63(66,69)cm ending with a P row.
Next row. Cast off 22(28,31) sts, K until 22(28,31) sts rem, place the 32(32,34) sts just worked onto a holder, cast off to end.

FRONT

Work as given for Back as far as *.
Change to 5mm needles and st. st. and work straight to a total measurement of 51(53,56)cm ending with a P row.

Shape neck.
Next row. K30(36,40), turn, P2 tog tbl, P to end.
** Working on these sts only, dec 1 st at neck edge only on next 3 rows, then on next 4(4,5) alt rows. (22,28,31 sts rem.)
Work 13 rows straight, ending with a P row, and with armhole edge the same length as that on the Back.
Cast off. **

Rejoin yarn to inside edge of rem sts, K16 sts and place them on a holder, K to end.
Next row. P to last 2 sts, P2 tog.
Repeat from ** to **.

NECKBAND

Press according to ball band instructions.
Join left shoulder seam. With 4mm needles, and with right side facing, pick up and K the 32(32,34) sts from the back neck holder, 24(24,25) sts down the left neck slope, 16 sts from the front neck holder and 24(24,25) sts up the right neck slope. (96,96,100 sts.)
Work 8 rows in K2, P2 rib.
Cast off in rib.

ARMBANDS

Join rem shoulder seam.
On the Front and Back, at each side, mark a point 25(28,30)cm down from the shoulder seam.
With 4mm needles and with right side facing, pick up and K 92(100,108) sts between these two points, up one armhole edge and down the other.
Work 8 rows of K2, P2 rib.
Cast off in rib.

TO MAKE UP

Join all rem seams.

For pattern see page 71

For
pattern
see page 77

COTTON
TOP

COTTON TOP

(Colour illustration, page 76)

A pretty cotton top with a very simple lace pattern is ideal for the young or young at heart. It has a round neck and set-in puff sleeves.

MATERIALS

Lister Bamboo Plain
Bright Pink (787)   9   10   10 × 50g balls

1 pr 4mm (No. 8) needles
1 pr 3¼mm (No. 10) needles
1 pr 3mm (No. 11) needles.

MEASUREMENTS

To fit	76–81	86–91	97–102 cm
	30–32	34–36	38–40 in.

TENSION

22 sts and 28 rows = 10cm (4in.) in stocking stitch on 4mm (No. 8) needles.

BACK AND FRONT [Both alike]

With 3mm needles, cast on 92(104,114) sts and work 4cm in
K1, P1 rib, inc by 1 st at end of last row. (93,105,115 sts.)
Change to 4mm needles and lace-stitch pattern as follows:
Starting with a K row, work 7 rows in st. st.
K 1 row.
Next row. K1, (yon, K2 tog) to end.
K 1 row.
Rep these 10 rows throughout rem of work.
Work straight in lace-stitch pattern to a total length of at least
28cm ending with the 10th row of the pattern.

Shape armholes.
Keeping lace-stitch pattern correct throughout, cast off 5(5,6) sts
at beg of next 2 rows.
Dec 1 st at each end of next 5 rows, then every alt row until
69(75,81) sts rem.
Work straight until armholes measure 14(17,19)cm, ending with
a wrong side row.

Shape neck, continuing to keep pattern correct.
Next row. Work 19(22,25) sts, turn, P2 tog tbl, work to end.
★★ Working on these sts only, dec 1 st at neck edge only on next
6(7,8) rows. (12,14,16 sts rem.)
Work 3(2,1) rows straight.
Cast off.★★
Rejoin yarn to inside edge of rem sts.
Work 31 sts and place them on a holder, work to end.

Next row. Work to last 2 sts, P2 tog.
Repeat from ** to **.

SLEEVES

With 3mm needles, cast on 66(74,82) sts and work 4cm in
K1, P1 rib.
Next (increasing) row. * Rib 1 st, inc 1 st in next st in rib*, rep
from * to * to end. (99,111,123 sts.)
Change to 4mm needles and lace-stitch pattern as given for the
Back and work straight to a total measurement of 10(11,11)cm
ending with a wrong side row.

Shape top, keeping lace-stitch pattern correct throughout.
Cast off 5(5,6) sts at beg of next 2 rows, then dec 1 st at each end
of the next 5 rows.
Dec 1 st at each end of every alt row until there are 39(39,43) sts.
Work 1 row, so ending with a P row.
Next row. K1, (K2 tog) to end. (20,20,22 sts.)
Cast off.

NECKBAND

Join left shoulder seam.
With 3¼mm needles, and with right side facing, pick up and
K 11(11,12) sts down the back right neck slope, the 31 sts from
the back neck holder, 11(11,12) sts up the left back neck slope,
11(11,12) sts down the left front neck slope, 31 sts from the front

neck holder, and 11(11,12) sts up the right front neck slope.
(106,106,110 sts.)
Work 8 rows of K1, P1 rib.
Cast off in rib.

TO MAKE UP

Do not press.
Join remaining seams matching all pattern and shaping, and
easing sleeve head fullness into the top of the armhole.

MOHAIR DIAGONAL JUMPER

MOHAIR DIAGONAL JUMPER

(Colour illustration, page 57)

A soft luxurious Mohair which comes in lots of lovely colours, makes this beautiful, but easy-to-knit jumper. It has a round neck and simple dropped shoulder line, with the Back and the Front divided diagonally into two colours, arranged so that they match at the side seams, with each sleeve in a different colour.

MATERIALS

Lister Tahiti 5-Star Mohair

Purple (684)	8	8	9 × 25g balls
Pink (709)	8	8	9 × 25g balls

1 pr 5mm (No. 6) needles
1 pr 4mm (No. 8) needles.

MEASUREMENTS

To fit	76–81	86–91	97–102 cm
	30–32	34–36	38–40 in.

84

TENSION

16 sts and 22 rows = 10cm (4in.) in stocking stitch on 5mm (No. 6) needles.

BACK

With 4mm needles and purple, cast on 68(76,84) sts and work 5cm in K2, P2 rib.★
Change to 5mm needles and st. st. and work as follows:
Next row. K2(6,10) sts in pink, K to end in purple.
Next and every alt row. P all sts in the same colour as they were on the previous row.
Next K row. K3(7,11) sts in pink, K to end in purple.
Next K row. K4(8,12) sts in pink, K to end in purple.
Continue in this way, working one more st in pink on every K row, until only 2(6,10) purple sts rem.
P 1 row, working all sts in the same colours as on the previous row.
Next row. Working all sts in the same colours as on the previous row, cast off 20(24,28) sts, K until 20(24,28) sts rem, and place the 28 sts just worked onto a holder.
Cast off to end.

FRONT

Work as given for Back as far as ★.
Change to 5mm needles and st. st. and work as follows:
Next row. K66(70,74) sts in purple, K rem 2(6,10) sts in pink.

Next and every alt row. P all sts in the same colour as they were on the previous row.

Next K row. K65(69,73) in purple, K rem 3(7,11) in pink.

Next K row. K64(68,72) in purple, K rem 4(8,12) in pink. Continue in this way, working one more st in pink on every K row, until 12(16,20) purple sts rem.

P 1 row, continuing to keep colours correct.

Shape neck.

Continuing to keep colours correct and to work one more pink st on every K row, work neck shaping as follows:

Next row. K27(31,35), turn, P2 tog tbl, P back.

★★ Working only on these sts, dec 1 st at neck edge only on next 2 rows, then on next 4 alt rows. (20,24,28 sts rem.)

Work 8 rows straight, ending with a P row on which 2(6,10) sts are purple.

Cast off in the same colours.★★

Rejoin pink yarn to inside edge of rem sts, K14 sts and place them on a holder, K to end.

Next row. P to last 2 sts, P2 tog.

Rep from ★★ to ★★ but in pink only.

SLEEVES

Make one in pink and one in purple.

With 4mm needles, cast on 36(36,40) sts and work 5cm in K2, P2 rib.

Change to 5mm needles and st. st., and inc 1 st at each end of every 4th row until there are 72(76,80) sts.
Work straight to a total measurement of 46(46,48)cm or desired length to underarm, ending with a P row.
Cast off loosely.

NECKBAND

Do not press or brush.
Matching colours, join left shoulder seam.
With 4mm needles, using pink, pick up and K the 28 sts from the back neck holder, 15 sts down the left neck slope, 14 sts from the front neck holder, and 15 sts up the right neck slope.
(72 sts for all sizes.)
Work 4cm in K2, P2 rib.
Cast off in rib.

TO MAKE UP

Join all rem seams in matching colours, with the purple sleeve as the left sleeve and the pink sleeve as the right, thus matching sleeve colour to armhole colour and ensuring that armholes are 23(24,25)cm deep after making up.

BABY'S JACKET

BABY'S JACKET

(Colour illustration, page 95)

Traditional baby jackets are ideal garments to make if you are just learning to knit, or if you are beginning to knit again after a long time. This one is as easy as possible and is in simple garter stitch with a full skirt and straight sleeves set into square armholes.

MATERIALS

Lister Baby Supersoft 4-ply
Turquoise (18)   2   3   3 × 40g balls

1 pr 3¼mm (No. 10) needles
1 pr 2¾mm (No. 12) needles
3(4,4) buttons.

MEASUREMENTS

To fit	41	46	51 cm
	16	18	20 in.

TENSION

28 sts and 36 rows = 10cm (4in.) in stocking stitch on 3¼mm (No. 10) needles.

MAIN PIECE [Make one]

With 3¼mm needles, cast on 214(238,262) sts and work straight in garter stitch (every row K) until work measures 13(13,15)cm.
Next (decreasing) row. (K2 tog) to end. (107,119,131 sts.)
K3 rows.

Divide for armholes.

Continuing in garter stitch, K25(28,31), cast off 5 sts, K until 30(33,36) sts rem, cast off 5 sts, K rem sts.

Right Front.

Working on this last group of 25(28,31) sts, ★ work 6(8,8)cm straight in garter stitch, ending at outside (neck) edge.

Shape neck.

K7(7,8) sts and place them on a holder, K to end.
Dec 1 st at neck edge on next 4 rows, then on each alt row twice.
(12,15,17 sts rem.)

Shape shoulder.

K2 rows, so ending at armhole edge.
Cast off 6(8,9) sts at beg of next row.
K1 row.
Cast off rem 6(7,8) sts. ★

Rejoin yarn to right armhole edge of centre (back) 47(53,59) sts and continue on these sts in garter stitch until back measures same as right front to shoulder.

Cast off 6(8,9) sts at beg of next 2 rows, then 6(7,8) sts at beg of next 2 rows, place rem 23(23,25) sts on a holder.

Left Front.
Rejoin yarn to inside armhole edge of rem sts and work buttonhole row as follows:
K to last 4 sts, yon, K2 tog, K2.
Work as for right front from * to *, but, repeating this buttonhole row every 2½cm, so working 3(4,4) buttonholes in all before the front measures 6(6,8)cm.
Complete neck and shoulder as given for right front, so reversing shapings.

SLEEVES

With 2¾mm needles, cast on 34(36,38) sts and K 4 rows.
Change to 3¼mm needles and continue in garter stitch, inc 1 st at each end of every 4th row until there are 40(46,46) sts.
Work straight to a total measurement of 13(15,20) cm.
Mark this point.
K 5 rows.
Cast off loosely.

NECKBAND

Do not press.
Join both shoulder seams. With 2¾mm needles and with right side facing, pick up and K the 7(7,8) sts from the right front

neck, 8 sts up the right neck slope, the 23(23,25) sts from the back neck holder, 8 sts down the left neck slope, and the 7(7,8) sts from the left front neck. (53,53,57 sts.)
P 1 row.
K 1 row.
P 1 row.
Cast off loosely.

TO MAKE UP

Join sleeve seams up to marked point. Insert sleeves, matching the undersleeve seam to the centre of the underarm, and the cast-off edge of the sleeve to the armhole sides.
Sew on buttons to match buttonhole positions.

For
pattern
see page 103

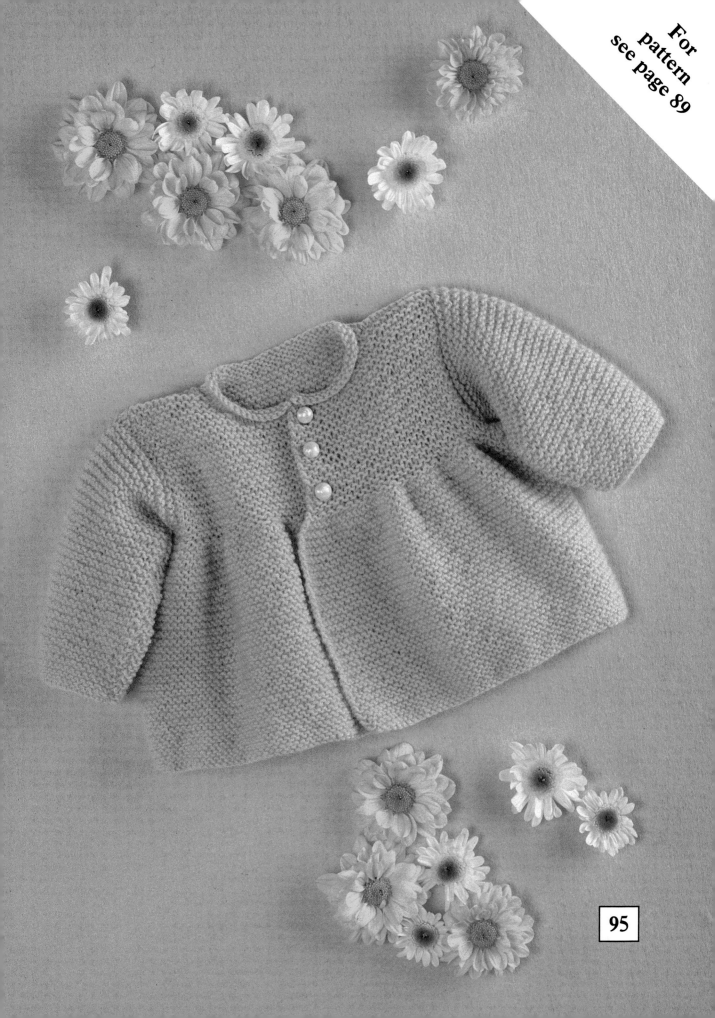

For pattern see page 89

95

For
pattern
see page 97

TEDDY

TEDDY

(Colour illustration, page 96)

Knitted bears are quite the nicest, most cuddly, squashable, washable bears of all. This bear is quickly made in a brushed, chunky yarn and will have a character all his own. Cheap to make, at a fraction of the cost of a posh shop bear, children will love him and he will be the success of the day at the bazaar.

MATERIALS

Lister Libra Brushed Fashion Chunky
White (106)   1 × 100g ball.
Note. Teddy actually used approximately 60g, so 2 × 100g balls would make 3 teddies.

Approximately 150g washable toy stuffing.
1 – 16mm toy safety nose.
1 pr 16mm toy safety eyes or suitable buttons.
Length of ribbon for a bow.
1 pr 6½mm (No. 3) needles.

Safety Note. Always use safe, non-toxic, washable materials if toys are for small children, and stitch on any decorations, including ribbon.

MEASUREMENTS

The teddy is approximately 36cm (14in.) tall.

TENSION

14 sts and 20 rows = 10cm (4in.) in st. st. on 6½mm (No. 3) needles.

Use needles chosen for main tension and st. st. throughout, except where otherwise stated.

BODY [Make 2, both alike]

Cast on 11 sts and inc 1 st at each end of every row to 21 sts.
Work 11cm straight.
Dec 1 st at each end of every row to 11 sts.
Cast off.

LEGS [Make 2, both alike]

Cast on 20 sts and work 10cm straight, ending with a P row.
★ **Next row.** (K2 tog) to end.
Next row. P.
Rep from ★ once, then run a thread through rem 5 sts and leave a long end.

ARMS [Make 2, both alike]

Cast on 2 sts and inc 1 st at each end of every row to 20 sts.
Work 5cm straight ending with a P row.
Work as given for legs from * to end.

HEAD

Cast on 30 sts and inc 1 st at each end of every alt row to 42 sts.
Work 2 rows straight.
Dec 1 st at each end of every row to 16 sts, then every alt row to 2 sts.
Work 2 tog, cast off.

EARS [Make 2, both alike]

Cast on 4 sts * and inc 1 st at each end of 2nd row. (6 sts.)
Work 2 rows straight.
Dec 1 st at each end of next row. (4 sts.) *
Work 1 row.
Rep from * to *, cast off.

TO MAKE UP

Brush all pieces on the st. st. side. Seam body halves together and stuff. Seam legs, stuff and attach, with ends closed, to bottom of body. Seam, stuff and attach arms open-ended to shoulders. Seam side edge of head to form a centre front seam.

Bring point of head to the top of the nose and join the resulting Y-shaped seam. Insert safety eyes and nose if used. Slightly gather the neck opening, stuff and attach head with neck open. Double ears, seam and attach. Embroider remaining features and stitch on ribbon bow.

DOLLS

DOLLS

(Colour illustration, page 94)

The dolls here are both knitted from the same pattern, but the larger doll is knitted in double-knitting yarn, and the smaller doll is knitted in 4-ply. The pattern can be used for any yarn using suitable needles for that yarn, but the doll will vary in size, of course, according to the thickness of the yarn. The 4-ply doll is a schoolgirl in basic grey and red, and her double-knitting friend has her blue party dress on. You can choose whether to make a simple or frilled dress and, of course, you can choose any colours you like for this basic pattern.

If you prefer, the clothes can be removable, but whatever materials or fastenings you use, do be sure that they are all non-toxic, safe and firmly attached.

MATERIALS

In both double-knitting and 4-ply, less than a 50g ball of the main skin colour and the main dress colour is needed, plus scraps of chosen colours for socks, shoes and pants, and scraps for hair and embroidery of features. Used here are Lister Richmond double-knitting and Lister Richmond 4-ply. Also needed are a small quantity of washable toy stuffing and any ribbons and buttons for decoration, plus a short length of elastic.

MEASUREMENTS

The 4-ply doll is approximately 28cm (11in.) tall.
The double-knitting doll is approximately 36cm (14in.) tall.

TENSION

In 4-ply, 28 sts and 36 rows = 10cm (4in.) in st. st. on
3¼mm (No. 10) needles.
In double-knitting, 24 sts and 32 rows = 10cm (4in.) in st. st. on
4mm (No. 8) needles.
Use needles chosen for main tension and st. st. throughout,
except where stated.

LEGS [Make 2, both alike, in skin colour]

Cast on 14 sts and, starting with a K row, work 42 rows.
Next row. (K2 tog) to end.
Next row. P.
Next row. K1, (K2 tog) to end.
Run a thread through rem sts and use to seam up.

BODY HALVES [Make 2, both alike, in skin colour]

Cast on 20 sts and, starting with a K row, work 8 rows.
Dec 1 st at each end of next then every other row to 14 sts.
Work 1 row.
Inc 1 st at each end of next and every foll 4th row to 20 sts, then
work 14 rows straight.

Cast off 3 sts at beg of next 4 rows.
Work 1 row, then cast off.

HEAD [Make 1 in skin colour]

Cast on 16 sts and starting with a K row, work 2 rows.
Next row. (Inc 1 st in next st, K2, inc 1 st in next st) 4 times.
Next row. P.
Next row. (Inc 1 st in next st, K4, inc 1 st in next st) 4 times.
(32 sts.)
Work 15 rows straight, ending with a P row.
Next row. (K2 tog, K4, K2 tog tbl) 4 times.
Next and every alt row. P.
Next K row. (K2 tog, K2, K2 tog tbl) 4 times.
Next K row. (K2 tog, K2 tog tbl) 4 times.
Next K row. K2 tog to end and run a thread through rem sts.

HANDS AND ARMS [Make 2, both alike, in skin colour]

Cast on 2 sts and inc 1 st at each end of every K row to 14 sts.
Work 21 rows straight, ending with a P row.
Next row. (K2 tog) to end.
Next row. P.
Next row. K1, (K2 tog) to end and run a thread through rem sts.

DRESS [Made in one piece in chosen colours]

For a frill: Cast on 176 sts * and K4 rows.
K1 row then P1 row.
Next row. (K2 tog) to end. * (88 sts.)

For a straight edge: Cast on 88 sts and K 5 rows.

Both versions.

Work 27 rows starting with a P row.
Next row. To make waist, (K2 tog) to end. (44 sts.) Change colour here if desired.
Work 15 rows.

Divide and shape armholes.

Next row. Work 11 sts, turn and work a further 9 rows on these sts, cast off.
Rejoin yarn to rem sts with right side facing and K22, turn and work a further 7 rows on these sts.
Next row. K6, K2 tog tbl, turn, P2 tog tbl, P to end, cast off.
Rejoin yarn to rem 14 sts, cast off 6, K2 tog, K to end.
Next row. P to last 2, P2 tog.
Cast off.
Rejoin yarn to rem 11 sts with right side facing, and work 10 rows on these sts.
Cast off.

SLEEVES [Make 2 in chosen colour]

For a frill: Cast on 32 sts, and work as for main piece of dress from * to *. (16 sts.)

For a straight edge: Cast on 16 sts and work 4 rows of K1, P1 rib.

Both versions.
Change to st. st. and work 16 rows, then cast off.

PANTS [Make 2, both alike, in chosen colour]

Cast on 24 sts and work 3 rows in st. st. starting with a K row.
Next row. K.
Work 15 rows straight starting with a K row.
Next row. K.
Work 3 rows straight starting with a K row, then cast off.

SOCKS/SHOES [Make 2, both alike]

Cast on 18 sts in chosen colour for rib top and work 4 rows in K1, P1 rib.
Change to st. st. and chosen sock colour and work 12 rows, starting with a K row.
Work 4 further rows of shoe colour if desired.
Next row. (K2 tog) to end.
Next row. P.
Next row. K1, (K2 tog) to end and run a thread through rem sts.

TO MAKE UP

Seam body halves together and stuff. Seam arms and legs leaving top ends open, stuff and attach open-ended.
Seam head, stuff and attach. Join shoulder seams on dress. Seam and insert sleeves, put dress on doll and seam up the back, or, if preferred, fasten with press fasteners, or buttons and button loops. Seam socks/shoes. Fold in half pants halves, seam 1cm inside leg seams, then front and back seams. Turn hems onto wrong side and loosely slip stitch down. Thread elastic in waist hem. Embroider features. Cut lengths of yarn for hair, stitch on and style as desired. Add any other desired decoration.

CRESCENT

— LARGE PRINT —

For those who appreciate the advantages of a larger than usual print.

CRESCENT books are available both in hardcover and paperback, with such popular authors as Rosemary Anne Sisson, Brian Johnston and Tessa Barclay. This varied list includes Historical Fiction, Romance, Thrillers and Non-Fiction, with two to three titles published every month.

ACTUAL
SIZE
OF PRINT

CHAPTER VI

Festival of Knaves

To Polly Fitch, what she had glimpsed of Whitehall Palace on her way to the small chambers she had been given, was a bewildering labyrinth. Long corridors, all looking much the same to her, with their portraits and their gilded furniture and their gigantic candelabra, intersected unexpectedly; panels swung open to reveal hidden doors; twisting staircases secretly linked floor with floor, narrow passageway with narrow passageway. Everywhere there was a constant press of

CRESCENT LARGE PRINT
—— FICTION ——

A story of life in the early days
of the Archers, as rural
Ambridge slowly recovers from
the effects of the First
World War.

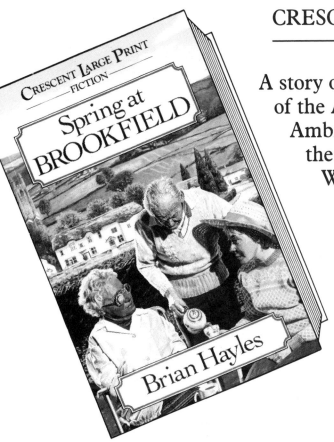

CRESCENT LARGE PRINT
—— HISTORICAL ——

Rosemary Anne Sisson's tale
of love between the French
widow of Henry V and Owen
Tudor. With their love came
the start of the Tudor
dynasty in England.

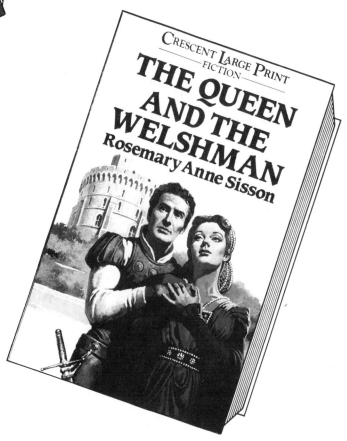

CRESCENT LARGE PRINT
─── SHORT STORIES ───

An anthology of twelve short stories by some of the finest women writers in the English language, including Agatha Christie, Iris Murdoch and Bernice Rubens.

CRESCENT LARGE PRINT
─── CRIME ───

A collection of twelve rare adventures of Sir Arthur Conan Doyle's great detective.